Our Times
in Rhymes

Sam Leith

Sam Leith is the literary editor of *The Spectator* and a columnist for the *FT*, whose work has appeared in *The Times*, *Guardian*, *TLS* and *New York Times* among other outlets. He's the author of several books, including *You Talkin' To Me? Rhetoric from Aristotle to Obama* and *Write To The Point: How To Be Clear, Correct and Persuasive on the Page*.

Edith Pritchett

Edith Pritchett is the resident cartoonist for slow news publisher Tortoise. She won the Cape Graphic Short Story Prize in 2018. She brings a Posy Simmonds-like wit to the preoccupations of the millennial era.

Our Times in Rhymes

Being A Prosodical Chronicle of Our Damnable Age

Sam Leith

Illustrations by Edith Pritchett

■ SQUARE PEG

1 3 5 7 9 10 8 6 4 2

Square Peg, an imprint of Vintage,
20 Vauxhall Bridge Road,
London SW1V 2SA

Square Peg is part of the Penguin Random House group of companies
whose addresses can be found at global.penguinrandomhouse.com

Penguin
Random House
UK

First published by Square Peg in 2019

Penguin.co.uk/vintage

A CIP catalogue record for this book is available from the
British Library

ISBN 9781529110197

Typeset in 13/18.5 pt Adobe Caslon Pro Regular
by Integra Software Services Pvt. Ltd, Pondicherry

Printed and bound in Great Britain by Clays Ltd, Elcograf S.p.A.

Penguin Random House is committed to a sustainable future for our
business, our readers and our planet. This book is made from Forest
Stewardship Council® certified paper.

MIX
Paper from
responsible sources
FSC® C018179

To Bill, with gratitude

Contents

Introduction

What kind of book is this one in
  your hand?
A book in which I use my inner ear
To seek to understand
  The Brexit year.

I try to catch the spirit of the times.
I run the gamut: angry, then despairing.
There's jokes, some iffy rhymes
  And swearing.

My pitch to casual readers isn't soppy.
It's hardback, and it costs a modest sum
So go on. Buy a copy
  For your mum.

January

They named the year's first month after a
    two-faced Roman god,
With one face on the future and the other on
    the past.
Adieu the even-numbered year, well met (we
    hope) the odd;
The Brexit year, the year in which the nation's die
    is cast.
We pledged to go two years back, though; we're
    going nowhere fast.
Two years at Brussels' buffet, and lean pickings on
    the plate;
Still, at least – we could console ourselves – we're
    having a debate.

So gammons shrieked at snowflakes and the
    snowflakes shrieked right back,
'You're thick!' 'You lost! Get over it!' 'So smug!' 'So
    sad!' 'You're bitter!'.
The death threat came, the pile-on, and the
    personal attack:

Less 'frank exchange of views', and more
  'repulsive row on Twitter',
While quantum futures flickered, alternating
  gloom or glitter.

We sneered about their 'unicorns', they sneered at
  our 'elites';

We cheered our pyrrhic victories and their
    meaningless defeats.

But still the clock ran down, alongside no-deal
    preparation –
A 'just-in-case', a 'belt-and-brace', a 'better we
    prepare' –
Which gave a laugh to citizens of every other
    nation.
Matt Hancock (yes, I know: who he?) was there
    to say 'There, there.
These daft prognostications are the fruits of
    Project Fear.
We don't need food or medicine – but even if
    we do,
I'm buying all the fridges in the world. We'll
    muddle through!'

But no-deal loomed and panic rose. So, hasty and
    belated,
They splashed the cash, went on the lash with
    sackloads of our groats.

(And fourteen million quid this stupid
    government donated
To a dodgy ferry company that hadn't any boats.)
Now even bullish Brexiteers were turning round
    their coats.
James Dyson (like that bloke from 'Spoons) had
    cheered for Leave before –
Yet promptly relocated his HQ to Singapore.

The CEO of Airbus wrote to warn we'd all go
    under
(as did Asda, Sainsbury's, KFC and Jaguar Land
    Rover),
Some prat MP went on TV and tore his note
    asunder.
And Project Fear said: 'Hold my beer. Before all
    this is over
There'll be twenty-mile lorry parks along the
    road to Dover.'
We stockpiled tins of vegetables, and thought the
    public good
Might be served by herding oldies into cellars for
    our food.

The vote approached. Our leaders sought to bully,
  beg, cajole.

'You'd best support my deal,' said May. 'For if you
  don't back me,

There'll be no deal and we'll be in a frightful
  bloody hole.'

She thought that threat had nailed it until
  someone said 'Yippee!':

The freedom-loving nutters in the so-called
  ERG.

'I mean,' she said, 'no *Brexit* if you don't support
  my deal.'

But then the wet Remainers gave a pre-orgasmic
  squeal.

On hearing that, Theresa May thought wanly:
  'That's me sunk.
The silly asses vote me down and we go crashing
  out.

I wonder if it's not too late for me to do a bunk:
When shit met fan my predecessor didn't hang
  about.
Perhaps I'll write *The Memoirs Of A Bloody
  Tricky Trout.'*
But thus far stepp'd in blood, and that: the
  captain stayed on deck
And got back to deckchair placement in the
  hours before the wreck.

And what had been foretold, of course, in due
    course came to pass:
The vote went just the way the pundits said that
    it would go.
And Corbyn saw a chance, at that, to kick the
    PM's arse –
And true to form he swung and true to form he
    stubbed his toe.
And nothing changed and no one went and still
    we didn't know
Which if any of these many baleful outcomes was
    in store,
And we wondered what the hell this vaunted
    sovereignty was for.

A few of us got thinking there might be another
    way.
The States was still 'shut down' while Donald
    sulked about his wall,
But the world spun on regardless and the sun
    rose every day.
And most of the electorate was fond in its recall

Of how long Belgium did without a government
at all.
In bread-and-circus news, meanwhile, the nation
swallowed whole
Piers Morgan's condemnation of a vegan sausage
roll.

In Norfolk, out near Sandringham, they
summoned the police:
A celebrity collision with a hint of 'them and us'.
A benefit-dependent long-term immigrant from
Greece
Was found at fault, but not a single Leaver made
a fuss.
(You'd think they'd think of something for a
slogan on a bus.)
With the D of E's apology, the story went away,
And Philip lived to drive without a belt another
day.

That two-faced God I started with now reads as
metaphor:

The Hobson's Choice before us to be angry or be
cross;
The mithering and dithering, the hopeless 'either/
or'.
The recent past's a Whitehall farce, the future's a
dead loss.
We risked it (thank you, Kipling) on one turn of
pitch-and-toss!

We dared the world, should our luck fail, to kick
   us in the groin –
And calling 'Tails we win!', we flipped a double-
   headed coin.

February

*S*o February brought us low, and not just with
 its weather,
But apprehension; and, of course, the enervating
 way
Our leaders spouted empty vows to 'bring us back
 together'.
If only there'd been something to alert Theresa
 May
That the best-laid plans of mice and men so
 often gang agley.
Yes, February made us shiver, in its chilly rain,
In bouts of present tedium that augur future pain.

'Be bold! Be firm! Into the world!' they'd said
 before the vote –
Before the tangled legal lines we saw proliferate.
Now those we sent to Brussels had to strike
 another note:
'Redraft! Rejig! Oh f *** a pig: let's renegotiate!'

The Brexit that meant 'Brexit' now meant
    'subclause thirty-eight',
While the meaning of the backstop (as both sides
    ran down the clock)
Proved elusive as the Bandersnatch, the Snark or
    Jabberwock.

'Adieu, EU!' took more – who knew? – than one
    swipe of the paw.
The bluff and commonsensical cried 'Boo!' and
    'Bah! Unfair!'

Who knew that trade was complex? That our
    freedoms leant on law?
Who ever read the small print of *L'acquis
    communautaire*?
They stumbled quite amusingly when asked these
    things on air.
Historians of the future for whom Corn Laws are
    a doddle
Will find, surveying Spring this year, some stuff
    to tax the noddle.

Procedural contortions were a sight for all to see.
Amendment on amendment piled, like Pelion on
    Ossa.
Could this one split the difference? Or split the
    ERG?
Is this one from a sound MP? Well, that one's
    from a tosser!
At Spelman–Dromey, Cooper–Letwin, Saville
    Roberts, Costa,
The general public registered bewilderment at
    best.

(You'd have to understand them to be truly
    unimpressed.)

Then Donald Tusk got rather brusque. A 'special
    place in hell'
Awaited those, he said, who won a plebiscite with
    lies,
And flogged an easy Brexit that just wasn't theirs
    to sell.
Now very much debated was the 'Malthouse
    Compromise',
Which sounded like the sort of thing they show
    on Channel Five –
An action flick that sees Ben Affleck and
    Beyoncé Knowles
Flee cops round Alpine passes in a pimped-out
    Cooper–Boles.

But 'none shall pass', the Black Knight said in
    Python's *Holy Grail*,
And sure enough, none did – or not enough to
    break the tie.

Despairing of a process that seemed engineered
to fail
A clutch of Don Quixotes rode to combat, heads
held high.
And some said 'Brave!' and some said 'Finks!' and
most of us said: 'Why?'

I write their names out in a verse, these figures
    wrapped in myth:
Bold Berger, Coffey, Gapes, Umunna, Leslie,
    Shuker, Smith.

It's not exactly Yeats, I know: I work with what
    I've got.
But Luciana Berger gave the launch event some
    welly.
For fifteen minutes straight The Independent
    Group was hot.
A bold new force in public life had fire in its
    belly –
Fire doused, it seemed, quite easily, by going on
    the telly.
These knights errant that on the plain of politics
    were pricking
Cemented their undying bond at Nando's with
    some chicken.

Distracted from distraction by distraction we
    went on.

Some chose to shout the odds on whether
    Churchill was a shit;
A vicious white imperialist or wartime paragon.
The 'Momo Challenge' meanwhile gave the
    Daily Mail a fit –
While March the 29th drew nearer bit by
    dreadful bit.
The headlines were bananas. Like we'd give a
    good goddamn
That the PM let it slip she scrapes the mouldy
    bits off jam.

And soul by soul and silently our shining bounds
    decreased

As the Reaper plucked the eldest and the
brightest and the best.

K. Lagerfeld laid down his fan; R. Pilcher was
deceased;

A. Finney ceased to act; L. Radziwill was under-
dressed;

M. Falkender would list no more; A. Previn took
a rest.

J. Hardy, too, no longer teased our serious
 concerns.
He went unto the bourn from which no *News
 Quiz* guest returns.

And meanwhile, thirty million miles away in
 outer space
A lonesome friend who Brexited in 2003
Sent a telegram to Earth to say 'Goodbye, the
 human race'.
From a crater called Endeavour in the airless
 Martian sea
We heard the final status scan from Opportunity.
It kindled in all British hearts an empathetic
 spark:
'My battery is low,' the rover said. 'It's getting
 dark.'

March

W'd tried the courts, tried Parliament, so
    now came a petition:
The Europhiles, the trendy ones, the urban and
    the woke
Subscribed their names, and hoped to force a
    government admission
That the only course of action was by fiat to
    revoke,
Rejecting Brexit wholesale, saying no to pig and
    poke.
Six million signed, and we denounced as traitors
    and ingrates
The pedants pointing out the names traced back
    to Baltic States.

Remember *The Italian Job*? The villains end up
    stuck
On a cliff edge, like a see-saw, with a ton of
    stolen gold;
Retrieve the loot, at once you're overbalancing
    your truck,

And what comes next there's nobody who much
  needs to be told.
Yes, fortune favours 'still alive' before it favours
  'bold'.

Our Michael Caine was Farage, still all bonhomie
  and beer:
'Hang on a minute, lads,' said Nige, 'I've got a
  great idea.'

A March For Leave would show the world the
  strength of public rage:
A rally 'gainst the know-all Haves, by left-behind
  Have-Nots.
Betrayed! Elites! The People's Will! The Spirit of
  the Age!
From Sunderland to Hartlepool, from
  Middlesbrough to Notts,
An Army of the Common Man, all cross and
  banging pots.
The pitch was 'Want to show 'em?' and for anyone
  who did
You could join them on the public road for only
  fifty quid.

'The greatest march since Jarrow' was the Brexit
  Party line.
But far from seeing workers in their thousands
  downing tools
It more recalled a tea-shop queue in *Last of the
  Summer Wine*.
A washout in the drizzle. Still, the media, like
  fools,

Trained all their hungry cameras on five
gammons in cagoules,
And Nigel had a schedule clash, so couldn't walk
that far:
He dropped in for some photos but did most of it
by car.

A March To Stay was held, to counteract the
March For Leave:

A 'Put it to the People March'. A million souls
  were there
(Or so the organisers would have had us all
  believe);
Just think of all those panicked calls to nannies
  and au pairs!
They bunged up Whitehall, rammed Park Lane,
  thrombosed Trafalgar Square.
The flat-white drinkers of the metropolitan
  elite,
Outvoted at the ballot box, now voted with their
  feet.

Was this a sign the mood had changed, or
  something else at play?
They'd been more cunning, certainly, in setting
  out their stall:
They didn't, in the first place, ask participants to
  pay;
And they made the march a quickie, just a gentle
  Starbucks-crawl
To Parliament from Hyde Park – yes, most
  devious of all,

They marched in central London, which they had
   to know would mean
That no one had to travel very far from N19.

Mark Francois 'wasn't trained to lose'. (What was
   he trained to do?)
Mark Francois fights and dies before Mark
   Francois bends the knee.
He knows what he'd have done if he'd been here
   for World War Two:
Mark Francois owns a book about the fight for
   Normandy,
And has *Where Eagles Dare* on Blu-Ray and on
   DVD.
Those Fourth Reich EU bureaucrats, if bark
   should come to bite –
Mark Francois knew with certainty he'd beat
   them in a fight.

He stands as one example of how Brexit ultras
   thought:
'We're Spartans at Thermopylae, we're samurai,
   the Few,

Horatius at the Bridge, the Rorke's Drift
  Redcoats, those who bought
Their honour dear in blood to see the bloody
  business through.'

Instead of real combat, Brexit bluster had to do:
A psychic consolation prize for wars they never
　　fought;
A role-play Götterdämmerung for kids picked
　　last at sport.

And higher in the pecking order came the real
　　peckers:
The brains behind the brains behind the brains
　　behind the brainless.
They called themselves 'Grand Wizards' and they
　　motored up to Chequers
In vintage cars, with gleaming chrome and bonces
　　bright and stainless
To twist the PM's arm to say their Brexit could
　　be painless.
Hail Boris, Govy, Moggy, Davis, Raab, and
　　Smiffy too;
An awkward dinner party with the flavour of a
　　coup.

Did none of them beforehand have a google of
　　the name?

Did no one know 'Grand Wizard' is a trademark
  of the Klan
So 'Dark Lords of the Sith' would have been just
  about the same?
It didn't matter anyway. It all went down the
  pan:

They drove away as they'd arrived, with neither
   clue nor plan.
More sinister than all their pomp was to imagine
   this:
A world in which the world's in need of Iain
   Duncan Smith.

The chaos in the Commons rumbled joylessly
   along.
The votes which had been 'meaningful' were
   meaningful no more,
The word 'indicative' had almost never been so
   wrong.
The issues swirled like filth around a flooded
   toilet floor;
No plunger for these blockages of politics and
   law.
The DUP, the ERG, the blasted Irish border …
And ho, oh no!, it's John Bercow – with 'Order,
   order, oardaargh!'

So as the storied date approached, the natural
   climbdown came.

We had to kick the can again – extend rather
    than revoke:
A halting wayside breather for the lame led by
    the lame.
Dejected at the podium, the Maybot glitched and
    spoke
The not-quite punchline to a long, unfunny, not-
    quite joke.
We'll go – we hope – she said, before the
    European election;
Cold water splashed on Brexit's badly struggling
    erection.

So there we were in stasis, still reluctant to
    repent
The hubris that had led us to a far-from-tragic
    fall.
For history moves in hiccups, and the record
    shows we spent
Our vaunted 'Independence Day' a nation still in
    thrall:
We looked before we leaped and therefore never
    leaped at all.

It's like the bit in *Godot* where Vlad says to
  Estragon:
'We'll go?' 'Let's go,' reply comes. Hours later
  neither's gone.

April

The cruellest month, when longen folk to be
    in England now:
That's what they say of April in my books of
    English verse.
Perhaps the ancient rhythms of the year remind
    us how
Untroubled by our strife's the vast indifferent
    universe,
Where Fortune's wheel rotates and where the
    imp of the perverse
Applies to mortal hubris cosmological perspective –
Which for all but dear Piers Morgan is a
    humbling corrective.

In Galaxy M87 – deep space, only further –
They found a massive new black hole and
    photographed its face:
Just like the Eye of Sauron, to the casual observer.
An object of grave beauty, of annihilative grace
Which outstrips in destructive force 'most
    anything in space.

It's gravity's so powerful it sucks in waves of light;
Still, Mark Francois is confident he'd take it in a
    fight.

While back on Earth (for what it's worth), an
    enterprising teen
Named Greta Thunberg made the speech that
    launched a thousand tweets,

A pigtailed Jeremiah for our doomed
    Anthropocene.
In a last Hail Mary pass before the planet
    overheats
Extinction Rebels bunked off school and flooded
    through the streets.
'We're doomed!' they wailed. 'The signs are there
    for those with eyes to see 'em,'
And staged a Die-In at the Natural History
    Museum.

The public filled the cinemas to see the last
    Avengers:
Balm not in Gilead but in a big-screen fantasy

Where heroes with a finger-click could undo
    time's revenges,
Bring back the dead, and heal the world. Your
    worst anxiety
Was guessing when to sneak out in the middle
    for a pee.
But waiting on the street outside the Empire,
    Leicester Square,
Was far more of reality than humankind can bear.

Take UKIP, with the slate of unbelievable
    grotesques
It pushed for public office in the looming Euro
    polls.
They dreamed that one day soon, installed in
    Brussels at their desks,
We'd find the very cream of Britain's bedroom-
    dwelling trolls:
A bloke who made his dog salute 'Sieg Heil' for
    edgelord lols,
And 'Sargon' (or Carl Benjamin), a bearded
    jackanapes

Who proudly used Free Speech to say which
women he would rape.

The Brexit Party, also known as UKIP 2.0,
Was one more push to get the Farage clown-car
back in gear.
Well: folk like clowns and Farage rather more
than we had thought.
The Tories panicked. Polling seemed to justify
their fear
That the Brexit Party'd sweep them off the map
within a year.
But if you claim to hate elites, Nige, wouldn't it
be smarter
If your first prospective candidate's not called
Annunziata?

In a garden shed headquarters, meanwhile, up
East Finchley way,
The Labour leader brooded, and his face grew
ever paler.
He zeroed in upon the vital issue of the day –

By which he meant the need to find a reason for
the failure
Of the economic miracle of Marxist Venezuela.
'We ought to come out strong,' he said. 'It's just a
Zio plot.'
And Seumas said: 'Oh *Jeremy*!' And Jeremy said:
'WHAT?'

'But I'm against ALL forms of –' and his bagman
cut him off.

'Now, Jeremy. Let's try to – no, no. Not on
   Palestine.
On Brexit, right? They're getting wise to that
   strategic cough
You give when someone asks you the official
   party line.
If we can be "quite clear" and still say nothing,
   we'll be fine:
We leave, the Tories get the blame, Team Jeremy
   can't lose …'
'And if we do,' chirped Jeremy, 'we'll blame it on
   th—'
'FAKE NEWS!'

The Embassy of Ecuador announced that they
   were through
With the man that WikiLeaks regards as data's
   martyred saint.
But which of us won't weary of the sort of house
   guest who
Outstays his welcome hiding from a criminal
   complaint

And redecorates his quarters using human poo as
   paint?
Assange was carted off in cuffs. His look of Julian
   Sands
Had given way to 'tramp who eats lasagne with
   his hands'.

Sing, too, of Gavin Williamson, the hapless
   Private Pike
Who shot his foot while trying to stab his
   colleagues in the back
With titbits, here and there, he thought the
   yellow press might like.
A leak inquiry followed and the pillock got the
   sack
When it turned out that he'd talked after a
   meeting to a hack.
He strove for Francis Urquhart, but he never got
   the trick of it
And lost his job while looking like an extra from
   The Thick of It.

But that's not what the rest of us remember
   April for.
This was the month that Notre-Dame de Paris
   caught on fire:
Not just an immolation but a poignant metaphor.
We play back in our minds the awful toppling of
   the spire –
In ashes now, alongside all of Nineveh and Tyre;
A monument that stood eight hundred years
   beside the Seine
To a European culture that will never come
   again.

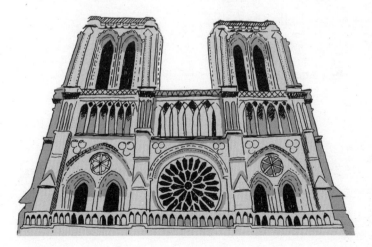

The flames caught slowly, first, but licked and
  quickened by and by.
The news spread out like smoke, and as devout
  Parisians learned,
They gathered on the trottoir underneath an
  orange sky.
Hands held, expressions marked with grief, and
  each face upward turned,
They sang 'Ave Maria' as the great cathedral
  burned.
There's silence in between the notes. In each eye
  something wells.
The bells, the bells, the bells, the bells, the bells,
  the bells, the bells.

May

*M*ay opened on a high note, and a rare
  reprieve from care:
The ancient tree of royalty was sprouting new
  green shoots.
The Duke of Sussex and his lovely bride had
  sprung an heir,
Whose name (they said) would incarnate the
  transatlantic roots
Of the offspring of Prince Harry and the fit one
  out of *Suits*.
So 'Ryder Cup Mountbatten-Windsor' could
  have been his name;
Instead they called him Archie, which struck
  critics as a shame.

Rejoicing, though, was general, and peals of bells
  rang out.
We warmed to see the infant introduced to good
  Queen Bess;
At last Prince Archie gave us something nice to
  talk about.

But soon enough the caravan was trundling on,
and yes:
The christening was private, disappointing the
Express.
Britannia's new-found rage and rancour didn't
long forsake her,
And when he sent a racist tweet we cancelled
Danny Baker.

Non-cordiale was the entente as May sat down
with Corbyn
Two years too late to see if they could find some
common ground.
As long as she'd been able the Prime Minister'd
ignored him
But – all her other options shot – mysteriously
found
That choirs that sing in unison make much the
sweeter sound.
Before the Euro-polls, of course, the talks went
down in flame,
And each one – who'd have thunk it? – gave the
other one the blame.

The campaign trail, for right-wing thugs, was
  fraught with new-found danger,
And Tommy so-called Robinson can testify to
  that:
Haranguing a town centre, he was bum-rushed
  by a stranger
With a novel type of protest, and the neo-Nazi
  prat
Just moments later wore a strawberry milkshake
  as a hat.

McDonald's closed their doors lest milkshake
  violence be done
But Burger King – free enterprise! – then offered
  two-for-one.

The Euro-polls approached, and Euro-optimists
  found grounds
For anti-Brexit parties to be fancying their
  chances.
But 'Lib-Dem surge' was every bit as thrilling as
  it sounds,
And as for others – after all their rallies and
  advances
The knights of Change UK returned to camp
  with broken lances.
A bold new stroke was needed, now, to get back
  in the game
And they resolved – third time's the charm! – to
  try another name.

Here was a poll on nothing much, an abstract
  thing to reckon:

Who'd represent the nation in a parliament we're
    leaving?
The candidates who swept to power were only
    there for wrecking
The proceedings of a chamber that not one of
    them believed in,
And set about insulting just as soon as being
    received in.
It goes to show how sourly our history repeats:
The best lacked all conviction while the worst
    were given seats.

What did it mean? It must mean *something*.
    Everybody swore
To implement that something with no moment
    of delay –
But each thought it meant just what each already
    thought before.
There was no doubt, for instance, in the mind of
    Mrs May:
It meant, she said, we must deliver Brexit right
    away.

And Labour (though their vote-share had been
pretty minuscule)
Declared it was a judgement on three years of
May's misrule.

But be that as it may, for Mrs May the times were
dark as
The times could get. Her goose was triple-cooked
(like chips) and gaily

The blue-rosetted vultures swooped to feast upon
her carcass.

Top hats flew ringwards: we had nearly three new
runners daily
In the race to seize the laurels worn by Gladstone
and Disraeli.
Churchillian was the oratory as each man tried
his luck:
'Fuck business!' 'Fuck fuck business!' (Fuck fuck
business? Fucking fuck.)

A certain flash of style was seen at least from
  Rory Stewart,
Not quite the Eton toff that some complacently
  assumed.
A meet-the-people tour on foot was how he
  chose to do it:
With shaky handheld camera up and down the
  isles he zoomed
And spoke good honest sense, which left his
  candidacy doomed.
'When I go to Afghanistan the local warlords
  rate me.
My Pashtun's pretty rusty, but will anyone debate
  me?'

If that seems pretty silly, better not to think
  about
The turmoil that one cycle of the news could put
  us through.
The PM hid in Downing Street refusing to come
  out,
While at the same time elsewhere – and I swear
  all this is true –

The chief whip had sought refuge from the media
  in a loo
And Nigel Farage couldn't do his rabble-rousing
  job
For hiding in his tour bus from a milkshake-
  toting mob.

Across the pond the angry tweeting tangerine
  reacted
To Robert Mueller saying that the Russians
  helped him win.
For even though the document was heavily
  redacted
(And Trump's Attorney General had done his
  best to spin
The line that it exonerated Donald Trump of sin)
The findings of the full report still threatened the
  illusion
Of the lumpenproletariat that there was 'NO
  COLLUSION!'

At first he said that Russia's tricks were not to do
  with him

And then he found an issue to put Mueller in the
    shade,
Declaring that he didn't for a second mean to
    swim
Against the pro-life zealots who had made
    another raid
On the freedoms that we'd thought were
    guaranteed by Roe v. Wade.
The liberal world was mortified to see the ugly
    clamour
To re-enact *The Handmaid's Tale* from Cork to
    Alabama.

The Champions League, at least, made British
    football fans less blue
When Liverpool, three points behind, their
    chances all but blown,
Beat Barcelona four–nil in the semis to go
    through.
A stadium in ecstasy like Anfield's never known:
A thousand thousand Scousers sang 'You'll Never
    Walk Alone'.

Then Tottenham, too, won through – to this
    unlikeliest of dreams:
A European Cup contested by two English
    teams.

And that is where we ended up – the old familiar
    story,
Of how, just as we tumble into history's last ditch,
There's refuge from reality in sport's symbolic
    glory.
When man makes plans, God laughs; and then
    He sends us something which
Gives all our hopes parodic shape upon the
    football pitch.
While Westminster broods on, no longer 'taking
    back control'
But hoping against hope for an eleventh-hour
    goal.

June

*I*t's getting worse. I swear it is. I write but as
    I find:
The end of the Anthropocene can hardly come
    too soon.
I don't think keeping track of this stuff's healthy
    for my mind;
Each month brings waxing lunacy with waning of
    the moon.
There must have been a reason Leighton called it
    Flaming June.
A presidential visit tied a bow upon the parcel
As the nation bent its knee towards the preening
    orange arsehole.

We didn't see diplomacy. I wonder if he's tried it.
He fixed on Meghan Markle and determined to
    abuse her:
He called her 'nasty' publicly and afterwards
    denied it.
Sadiq was next. The President told every Twitter
    user

The Muslim Mayor of London was a pint-sized
  'stone cold loser'.
This is the sort of banter that ambassadors will
  frown on;
Yet this one he did not deny but promptly
  doubled down on.

Her Majesty, of course, was forced to rise above
  and greet him
And he found absolutely the most graceless way
  to thank her

By presenting half his ghastly spawn when she
  came down to meet him.
The Cletus-looking twins and Princess Plastic-
  Face Ivanka:
Of course he brought the kids along, the
  nepotistic wanker.
Camilla couldn't quite resist a bat-squeak of a
  protest:
Her sarky wink went round the world as soon as
  people noticed.

Less subtle were the ways that normal folk set out
  to spoil it:
Contempt turned out as carnival, and filled
  Trafalgar Square.
A giant farting robot Trump was tweeting on the
  toilet,
And nappy-wearing Trump balloons were hoisted
  in the air ...
What good it did us (none at all) to know that we
  were there!
When asked about the protests, Trump came over
  hard of hearing

And said he'd noticed 'thousands' on the
pavements who were 'cheering'.

Good riddance, then, to Air Force One, good
riddance to the Beast.
They stopped in Ireland briefly for some
Guinness, golf and craic
Then lifted off again and headed briefly further
east
To honour those who perished in the Normandy
attack;
Which Donald did by signing his name biggest
on the plaque,
And using a war graveyard as a backdrop for his
face
Gave Fox an interview to call Pelosi 'a disgrace'.

The Women's World Cup soccer cheered the
punters up a lot.
We fell in love with glorious, pink-haired Megan
Rapinoe,
Whose US squad was everything their president
was not –

Before a White House invite came they said they
    wouldn't go.
It felt like more than football, then, each time we
    watched her throw
Her arms wide as if guiding planes to land on
    Airstrip One –
Part Boudicca, part Liberty and part Joan
    Hunter Dunn.

Are you on drugs? Well might you ask. But ask it
    no one had –
Until it came out Michael Gove had once been
    on cocaine.
Now candidates took turns to say that taking
    drugs is bad
But (so as not to look like squares) admitted, in
    the main,
They'd tried a puff of weed as kids but never
    would again.
Bhang lassi was Hunt's high point as a fancy-free
    young man;
And Rory Stewart, right on brand, smoked
    opium in Iran.

Each candidate mouthed bromides about
   'passion', 'plans' and 'vision'
And though the media had at least a
   semi-serious go
At presenting this fiasco as a national decision
A hundred thousand blue-rosetted seniors or so
Were the only ones whose votes were worth a
   pisshole in the snow.
In golf-club-gin-n-Jag-land, every Crispin, Sid
   and Doris

Thought 'best off out' and 'bloody rah', and 'like
    the sound of Boris'.

The 'sound of Boris' is what that man's girlfriend's
    neighbours heard
When the small hours saw the happy couple
    trading oaths and cusses.
She grabbed his laptop, red wine spilt and they
    swapped the absurd
Reproaches we may recognise from our domestic
    fusses.
(Perhaps she jogged his hand when he was
    painting wine-box buses.)
The nosy neighbours called the cops and further
    milked the caper
When they taped the whole damn shouting
    match and flogged it to a paper.

The man's a former colleague, so I speak with
    some affection
When I say I think him perfectly unsuited to the
    job.

He has a hack's quick cleverness and shifting of
   direction;
Puts hoof in mouth the moment that he opens up
   his gob;
Is thinking with his ego when not thinking with
   his knob.
On 'sovereignty' the fear's in me this opportunist
   clown
Will beggar all our children for a stupid abstract
   noun.

Yet vole nole, as the man himself would doubtless
   say,
A competition turned into a virtual coronation

And one by one the others were removed from
   field of play.
As came the hour no Gove would come to heal
   the broken nation;
And Rory walked – we never got to have that
   conversation.
There was a brief kerfuffle about tactics in the
   voting
But come the end of June it was all over bar the
   gloating.

And while we bickered, far away beside the Rio
   Grande
A photograph distilled the migrant spirit of the
   age:
A father with his daughter lying drowned upon
   the sand.
While Stormzy in a stab-vest on the Glastonbury
   stage
Gave vent antiphonally to a more parochial
   rage.

'Fuck Boris!' he exploded and the crowd took up
  the cry.
Its futile echo faded in the Glastonbury sky.

July

*T*he European Parliament commenced its
latest session,
With the Brexit Party's wretched raft of jut-
chinned MEPs.
Instead of setting out to make a favourable
impression
They thought to flick the frogs and wogs and
huns two-fingered Vs.
The attention-seeking creatures hit upon a
wizard wheeze:
In oafish ostentation, like a sullen little
boy,
Each turned his back in protest when they played
the 'Ode to Joy'.

Ann Widdecombe, her voice as high and
tremulous as ever,
Made the maddest maiden speech the Euro
Parliament had seen.
'Oppressed against oppressors' was the burden of
her blether.

As slaves against their masters, or as peasants in a
  scene
Of feudal revolution: such was Brexit held to
  mean.
No doubt it played quite well among the British
  gilets jaunes
While Strasbourg's proper MEPs rolled eyes and
  stifled groans.

And meanwhile, on July the Fourth, America
  gave thanks:

A #trumpparade to celebrate the #MAGA
  golden age.
And to this end, the Donald filled up
  Washington with tanks.
Had military flypasts, and in order to assuage
His ego, he demanded to be given centre stage.
He rambled about Space Force in a smirr of rain,
  and yup:
Most great was Donald's rage when almost
  nobody showed up.

His rage got greater still when it emerged that
  (Jesus wept!)
Our Man in Washington had called the President
  erratic,
'Dysfunctional', 'chaotic', 'incoherent' and
  'inept'.
The private memos Darroch wrote were truthful,
  if emphatic,
But splashed across the *Daily Mail* looked less
  than diplomatic.
Trump tweeted he was 'wacky' and a 'very stupid
  guy'

And shortly afterwards Sir Kim waved
  Washington goodbye.

Now Boris formed his Cabinet, and this one was
  a stormer:
Instead of 'Rt Hon', this lot – for Homeric
  epithet –
More often had their names preceded by
  'disgraced' and 'former'.
No disrespect intended to the ones not caught
  out yet,
But even offered decent odds, you'd hesitate to
  bet
That scandal for this gallery of rogues did not
  await us.
The old guard's duds were ruthlessly replaced
  with second-raters.

Take Raab, who didn't have a clue what Calais
  puts at stake,
Or Priti P's diplomacy, which merited a slap,
Or Williamson, whose slitherings defame the
  name of snake,

Matt Hancock, like a two-dicked dog at mention
   of 'an app',
And Leadsom, who's in all respects spectacularly
   crap.
The brown stuff rises too – and just as easily as
   cream.
If this lot are the dream-team then please wake
   us from the dream.

Dom Cummings runs things anyway. The PM's
   just a cog.

The commentator's task was now to guess what
    Dom would do.
For that – and *voi ch'entrate*, pals – you have to
    read his blog.
He trades in unminced words, amid a half-
    digested stew
Of quantum physics, polygenic theory and Sun
    Tzu.
A mystic and a hardnut, a thinker and a fighter,
Dom styles himself as Skeletor but several sigma
    brighter.

If Springheeled-Jack-the-Spad was master, Boris
    was the puppet.
Dom sent him to the country like a spaniel sent
    on walkies.
With nylon hair and yapping mouth, an amiable
    muppet
Whose cinematic heyday would have been before
    the talkies.
He waved a kipper in the air and told a bunch of
    porkies.

He promised us so many ways post-Brexit life
    would thrill us:
'The Mars bars won't run out!' and 'Drinking
    water might not kill us!'

And meanwhile, like a fever-dream, or memories
    that flit

Across the dimming minds of those Death puts
his mark upon,
The culture burped a modern spin on random
ancient shit.
There'd be a new *Blackadder*! *Carry On* would
carry on!
Lashana Lynch (who she?) was hotly tipped to
play James Bond.
A film of *Cats*! Remember that? And also –
who'd have thought? –
Miz Heather Mills, of noughties fame, was
cleaning up in court.

Just fifty years ago (since we are in nostalgic
mood)
Neil Armstrong first placed moonboot on the
surface of the moon
And people spoke of 'mankind', of a planetary
good.
The moment passed: as usual, the idealists spoke
too soon,
And the leaders who sought brotherhood
abruptly changed their tune.

We dreamed of going to the moon, and had the
    will to make it.
We dream no more. But who cares, eh, when
    modern tech can fake it?

The stories start to blur together. Can it really be
That Coco Gauff debated with Steve Bannon on
    Today?
That John McCririck's FaceApp stole Hong
    Kong's identity?

That Tommy Robinson and Katie Hopkins ran
away?
That fifty quid now features Alan Turing, who
was gay?
That as the nation sweltered in the welcome
summer sun
Hal Prince and Rutger Hauer went to Area 51?

Oh, summer's lease hath all too short a date! You
know the way
That sometimes, looking back, a hazy-weather
season seems
To telescope your memories into a single day?
A garden full of adults swapping back and forth
their screens:
The tennis and the cricket both reached thrilling
final scenes.
And drunk on wine and wild amazed we roared
aloud our gladness –
Then after, in the evening, came the chill and
creeping sadness.

August

$\mathcal{T}$he Donald in mysterious ways his wonders
    did perform.
He said he's months away from having AIDS
    and cancer cured
Then quoted with approval, in a sort of perfect
    storm
Of lunacy, a claim of his deserving to be called
The 'King of Israel' and the second coming of the
    Lord;
Then wroth he waxed when Denmark said that
    Greenland's not for sale.
If Trump is the Messiah then there's Kool-Aid in
    the Grail.

This penny-ante Pennywise who leads the USA
Thinks legal gun control's a thing that only
    pussies do;
Still thinks so after August brought two
    shootings in one day.
Now nine lay dead at Dayton. At El Paso twenty-
    two.

So down to the disaster with Melania he flew,
And rather than make laws that might help make
the killing stop
They grinned to camera with an orphaned baby
as a prop.

How fared the planet, meanwhile? Well, I'm glad
you asked because

'We're screwed' would be the precis of yours truly,
  'umble poet.
In Iceland they put up a plaque where once a
  glacier was,
And the Amazon was burning, not that most of
  us would know it.
(The information's there but Google doesn't want
  to show it.
In the infosystem of our turbocapitalist swindle
You type in 'Amazon' and 'Fire' and get an ad for
  Kindle.)

Some tried to set a good example. So, determined
  not
To add more carbon to the atmospheric overload
St Greta crossed the ocean on a solar-powered
  yacht,
Which might not save the planet, but it served –
  oh, joy – to goad
Some self-styled 'climate sceptics' to turn purple
  and explode.
Prince Harry's use of private jets was deemed by
  some immoral;

His brother showed him up by going FlyBe to
  Balmoral.

The princes' Uncle Andy had some problems of
  his own:
His old chum Jeffrey Epstein was about to come
  to trial,
And folk were pretty curious as to what the Duke
  had known.
He'd stuck by Epstein last time – after all, is none
  so vile
As can't extend forgiveness to a wealthy
  paedophile?
A photo from an Epstein party left a nasty taste:
A teenage girl with Andrew's chubby hand
  around her waist.

The Palace made a statement. It was not a very
  long one.
There'd been no 'extra pillows' on the freebies
  Andy took.
He was mortified to learn that his pal Jeffrey was
  a wrong 'un.

Like all the well-connected friends in Epstein's
   contacts book,
The prince had barely known him. Would that
   get him off the hook?
Then Epstein was found dead in jail. The web
   grew still more tangled:
He'd cleverly committed suicide by being
   strangled.

But there we leave that story, on the urging of our
    lawyers –
And turn instead to Britain's latest dismal Brexit
    clamour.
Reports were leaked that said a no-deal Brexit
    could destroy us.
They're 'out of date', insisted Gove, all squeaky
    and a-stammer,
Besides, it was the 'worst-case' plan, this so-called
    Yellowhammer.
Perhaps that's so, but I don't know – 'cause
    Michael, my old mate,
The documents you say are old are marked with
    this month's date.

Three-day delays at ports, and half a million
    cattle slaughtered;
The pound below the dollar; cancer patients
    dying early;
The streets awash with hooligans; the Union
    drawn and quartered;
Establishment of martial law – and 'mid the
    hurly-burly

The dreadful fear that corner shops run out of
    Curly-Wurly.
But still, we'll have blue passports – and the word
    from HMG
Is we'll mark our glorious freedom with a brand-
    new 50p!

And Boris, still all optimism, yelped: 'Wir
    schiffen das!'
Which brought a wintry smile to Merkel's sour
    old German puss.
It means 'we'll get this done'. He put his foot
    down on the gas.
Negotiation as a game of chicken: them or us.
Our dented Mini Cooper facing down a speeding
    bus.
And if he's levered out of Downing Street by Jez
    and Grieve?
His catspaws float the thought that he could just
    refuse to leave.

The no-deal crash-out plan for getting Brexit
    Britain free

Was gathering a dreadful sort of *faute-de-mieux*
  momentum,
With Dom 'n' Boris holding almost theologically
That the people's writ should run against the folk
  who represent 'em.
And faced with all those MPs so determined to
  prevent 'em,
The Leninists in Downing Street decided it was
  fitting
To neutralise the Commons by preventing it from
  sitting.

If Honourable Members would defy the people's
  will
They shamed (as many thought) the very benches
  that they sat in.
So the government determined to prorogue the
  House until
It offered no impediment. Now Boris closed the
  batting:
A bush-league *coup d'état* all prettied up with
  schoolboy Latin.
'Ne illegitamati! Quid pro quo! Id est! Ye gods!

Now Moab is my washpot and I wipe my feet on
    Dod's.'

Did Cabinet resist as they had promised to
    before?

Not weeks ago, and vocally, these ministers were
  avid
To rule out such an outrage. Men had died for us
  in war,
A misty-eyed Matt Hancock said. He said: 'I will
  not have it.'
'We're not selecting a dictator,' thundered Sajid
  Javid.
George Freeman called it 'bonkers'. Michael
  Gove thought it absurd.
Rudd called it 'the most extraordinary idea I've
  ever heard'.

A great deal of this sort of windy meretricious
  guff
Was spouted by frontbenchers when they didn't
  think he'd try it.
But come the actual prorogation, did they give a
  stuff?
I write their quotes down here to make it harder
  to deny it,
'Cause come the crunch in Cabinet they all went
  very quiet.

With only principle at stake, they'd boldly voiced
  their fears,
But now they wound their necks in just to further
  their careers.

September

*T*he new PM's majority of one was one under
    fire.
In military jargon these were blue-on-blue-on-
    blues
As Tory fought with Tory to bring Brexit to the
    wire.
Majority? That's Philip Lee; or was, until he'd
    choose
To cross the floor on live TV halfway through
    PMQs.
The PM gave a little grunt: You ain't seen
    nothing yet.
A parliamentary martingale, he doubled down his
    bet.

The moment that the votes were in he launched a
    charm offensive,
To show his solidarity with those who stood
    beside him.
He gave his troops a haircut: it was nothing too
    extensive.

Just kicked out all the twenty-one MPs who had
    defied him
(Pour encourager, all that jazz. The rebels: woe
    betide 'em.)
Majority of minus-god-knows-what – a
    masterstroke!
'Move fast and break things.' Yes indeed: he came,
    he saw, he broke.

The upshot of this strategy was *tout-a-fait* galvanic:
He asked them not to vote to bar no deal; and
    not to show
His no-deal homework to the public lest it make
    us panic.
He asked for an election, and they also told him
    no.
They'd voted seven times, and he'd lost seven in a
    row.
A rout? Disaster? No. Full house! What still
    escapes the press
Is Downing Street plays Yahtzee when you think
    it's playing chess.

The devastating countermove, the blazing
  winning streak –
Oh rest assured, they'd come. They only wanted
  you to think
They'd screwed the pooch bowlegged and were
  floundering up the creek.
These pratfalls were jujitsu moves, these injuries
  were fakes:
Karate Kid – not Sideshow Bob in a wilderness
  of rakes.

Embodying their sangfroid in the Commons was
  Rees-Mogg,

Who lounged in oafish torpor like a lizard on
  a log.

The intercession of St Jude (the saint of hopeless
  causes)
Might buoy up Catholic throwbacks, but the
  others upped and went,
Deserting the great ship of state like rats along
  the hawsers.
Jo Johnson (yes, his brother) had his fill and
  packed his tent,
And Amber Rudd made vocal protestation of
  dissent:
Called bullshit on 'we'll get a deal' and put the
  dagger in,
Denounced as 'vandalism' what the whips called
  'discipline'.

Nil desperandum, Boris thought. Majority? Pshaw!
Who needs MPs when – clever me – I've sent the
  House away?
And yet the Benn ('Surrender') Act had now
  passed into law,

Which if he cannot clinch a deal forces him to
   pray
To Europe – oh the shame of it – for three
   months' more delay.
He could defy the law before he'd let his project
   fail …
But most agreed that if he did he'd likely go
   to jail.

The PM set his stall out so that eight-year-olds
   would get it:
'By tattered purple trousers and the greening of
   my thumbs
These Euro-johnnies better watch their step or
   they'll regret it:
For something wicked out of Marvel comics this
   way comes.
The madder you make Hulk, my friends, the
   stronger Hulk becomes.
Red wine and blue resistance make Hulk's stores
   of rage grow fuller:
Hulk smash when Hulk get smashed! And Hulk
   shout: "Buller, Buller, Buller!"'

Hulk flew to Luxembourg next to discover if he
  mightn't
Embark upon a bold new diplomatic episode.
But when he heard protesters chanting, mighty
  Hulk got frightened,
And stayed indoors, revealing – when the rubber
  met the road –
That green-eyed monster wasn't Hulk, but
  quailing Mr Toad.
The show went on and laughter rained on
  Britain's empty chair:
A Q&A held jointly with the man who wasn't
  there.

A blessed break – but soon resumed the popgun
  and the cannon.
Yes, Corbyn was a 'chicken', David C. a 'girly
  swot',
The Benn Act a 'surrender bill' – which has the
  ring of Bannon,
The fash-adjacent strategist with whom he's
  thought to plot

LOCH NESS MONSTER

Instagram   Reality

(He says they've just swapped texts when people
   put him on the spot).
Whoever writes his rhetoric, transparent what it's
   for:
To make a vital national debate sound like
   a war.

In less exalted theatres, mind, they spin a similar
   line.

The notion of a 'female Bond' stuck in Piers
　　Morgan's throat:
'Not on my watch!' As if he's standing post in the
　　front line!
While telly cook James Martin struck a more
　　surreal note.
Some Fireman Sam-related 'PC bollocks' got his
　　goat.
His eejit face changed colour from boiled ham to
　　terracotta,
And he said he now identified – wait for it – as
　　an otter.

One Sarah Thomas crawled ashore in Dover,
　　tired and sopping,
Her feat a thing no human soul can fail to
　　admire.
She'd swum four times across the English
　　Channel without stopping.
She ought to make a packet as a swimming coach
　　for hire.

Long-distance front crawl is a skill we'll all need
   to acquire.
In confirmation, Thomas Cook, already on its
   knees,
Went bust, with many thousand Brits left
   stranded overseas.

The month saw three farewells of note – some
   short, some rather longer.
In death, a tyrant cheated justice one last time by
   stealth:
But when Mugabe cashed his chips, Zimbabwe
   danced the conga.
John Bercow said he'd go, who'd fought for
   Parliament's good health,
And in his closing speech paid touching tribute
   to himself.
John Humphrys left *Today*, too, after forty
   thousand years,
And everyone who'd raged at him now found
   themselves in tears.

The prorogation? Sorry, yes: that rumbled on as
    well.
Long story short, it went to court; the judges
    promptly squished
The fiction as to motive HMG had tried to sell.
The case – unanimous! – was all the plaintiffs
    could have wished:
This wasn't just judiciable but roundly was
    judished.
Amid the jubilation, though, the room contained
    an elephant:
That prorogation could turn out, in fact, to be
    irrelevant.

But any way you sliced it this was bad for the
    PM.
The spider Lady Hale wore had reeled in his
    fly.
Abroad, he was, in Washington (to flatter Trump
    pro tem),
But you could hear the high-pitched yelp from
    London if you'd try.

He called the Queen long distance and he
    gobbled humble pie
Then cut his trip short, bidding POTUS farewell
    with the look
Of one who wished he'd booked his homeward
    flight with Thomas Cook.

He'd lost those votes, pissed off the Queen and
    done something unlawful –
Not four weeks in, his Downing Street was
    poison, fire and fury.

An ill wind blew the PM, now, from north-
   north-west to awful.
As mayor he'd helped give public money to (so
   claimed the story)
A blonde US 'entrepreneur' called Jennifer Arcuri.
The nature of their 'friendship' drew the beady
   public eye,
When all at once a journalist said Boris groped
   her thigh …

October

'*G*et Brexit done' was now the line that
   Downing Street repeated.
Get Brexit done? Yes, very well – whatever *that*
   means. *Then?*
'Varadkar won't negotiate,' unnamed advisers
   bleated.
Belligerent self-pity was the tone from Number
   Ten,
And 'People versus Parliament' their plan for if
   and when
The next election happened. Oh, the goodies
   they've in store!
'Cry humbug!' to adapt the Bard. 'Let slip the
   dogs of war.'

Arcuri kept on being news. Would Boris come a
   cropper?
When asked about it on TV, the PM's face grew
   furious:
The boost he gave her businesses was only right
   and proper!

For her part, Miss Arcuri called the talk of nookie
   spurious:
He wasn't quite Arsexual, she hinted, just
   Arcurious.
She was his 'muse', his 'Everest', his 'Anne
   Boleyn'. It's funny:
She didn't even 'bang the dude', and still she got
   the money.

They'd gathered round her dancing pole for
   'lessons in technology',
The analogue then-mayor just needed help to
   get his hand in.

A leg-up, not leg-over; she was making no
  apology
For forming an 'intense bond' with a figure of his
  standing,
And though intense, their tête-à-têtes were in no
  way Ugandan
So nothing happened, got that? With which line
  drawn in the sand,
Her agent said she'd spill the beans for just two
  hundred grand.

While over stateside, Donny had some
  brainwaves for his wall,
Though most were not *completely* in compliance
  with the regs,
That is: a bit illegal and not very nice at all –
But who can make an omelette without breaking
  a few eggs?
Could border guards, he wondered, not shoot
  migrants in the legs?
And what about a water-hazard? Why not fill a
  trough
With snakes and hungry alligators? That would
  put them off.

But vultures circled. Tax returns, blackmailing the
  Ukraine,
Subpoenas, misdemeanours, grifts and cover-ups,
  hate speech ...
These tarry boulders piled up on his terminal
  moraine.
And Democrats, at last, got up the gumption to
  impeach
A president whose greedy grasp had long
  surpassed his reach.
But faced with solemn legal obligations, Donald
  tried to bluff:
The White House sent a letter saying Congress
  could get stuffed.

Distract, dismay, the playbook said, so Don
  picked up the phone.
Remember Syria? How the Kurds had stood with
  us before?
All bets were off now. Sorry, lads: afraid you're on
  your own.
'Cause loyalty goes both ways, so why shouldn't
  we withdraw?

You didn't help at Normandy in 1944.
With 'great and unmatched wisdom', Donald
  didn't care a jot:
Gave Erdoğan the go-ahead to kill the bloody lot.

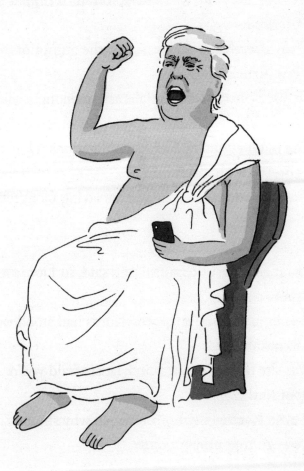

Perhaps that puts perspective on Prince Harry's
    new vendetta.
Enraged at how the papers had been covering
    his wife
He sued the *Mail on Sunday*, which had run a
    private letter;
Then after, for good measure, knowing back then
    it was rife
He used phone-hacking history to further twist
    the knife.
The public (who had bought those papers)
    cheered with gleeful malice;
But indications are they weren't so happy at the
    Palace.

By far the most delightful of the stories we saw
    run
Was how the trap snapped shut (or seemed to) on
    Rebekah Vardy.
Was she the rat who'd snitched her fellow WAGs
    out to the *Sun*?
Wayne Rooney's wife Coleen – Queen Wag –
    was getting proper mardy

Suspecting that some unnamed friend, disloyal
   and foolhardy,
Was flogging red tops stories from her private
   Instagram.
She planted false ones with RV, and ...
   Wagmageddon! Wham!

The Booker Prize saw London's Guildhall host
its annual dinner
For London's literati to dress up and then get
pissed. Oh,
But in this indecisive year they couldn't pick a
winner:
They shot for unanimity and evidently missed, so
Now Peggy Atwood shared the prize with Bernie
Evaristo.
This compromise could crock the prize, and
shames the judges too:
At least the Brexit vote was forty-eight to fifty-two.

And speaking of surprises, something very
strange took place:
For just as we thought Europe must have finally
lost patience,
The knot was quite uncuttable, and only to save face
Was Boris going on with all these sham
negotiations ...
A deal emerged, quite fully formed, confounding
expectations.
With less than two days left no one could say if it
would pass;

Still: who'd have thought that Boris would have
    pulled *this* out his arse?

But – whoops! – here was a border floating in the
    Irish Sea.
A number of those 'do-or-die' red lines had been
    rubbed out:
The terms were less important than the deal,
    apparently.
Reculer pour mieux sauter? You could think so –
    just about.
But many didn't, though the voting wasn't *quite*
    a rout.
The whipping operation marshalled, somewhat to
    its credit,
A hesitant alliance formed of those who hadn't
    read it.

That rush and bluster didn't wash with quite
    enough MPs
So still they lost, and back again we went to the
    beginning.
The Royal Mint stopped minting all those Brexit
    50ps,

And Number Ten, its bluff called (were they
    getting tired of winning?),
Dispatched the Benn Act's begging letter,
    furiously spinning
That though they'd sent it, two more sulky
    missives went behind it,
And – take that, Johnny Foreigner! – the PM
    hadn't signed it.

In Essex in a freezer truck police found thirty-
    nine
Dead bodies, smuggled migrants, mostly
    nameless Vietnamese
Whose hopes of a new life left them anonymous
    and dying.
Let scholars of the subject, while they suffocate
    and freeze,
Sift 'economic migrants' from the 'real refugees'.
Let demagogues make hay – ignore the desperate
    human toll
To incoherent fantasies of taking back control.

November

So Halloween had been and gone: the ghosts
    came in a barrage.
Westminster's paths were crossed by supernatural
    black cats,
And jack-o'-lanterns grinned and showed their
    teeth like Nigel Farage.

THE
NO-DEAL
PUMPKIN

The handmaidens of Hecate convened in pointed
  hats,
And from those Pugin ceilings dangled hordes of
  vampire bats.
A legislative Frankenstein received the Queen's
  assent
And danced the Monster Mash inside this
  zombie Parliament.

This time of year, the barrier between two worlds
  grows thin:
The veil of cobwebs opens momentarily to give
Safe passage to the spirit unappeased and
  peregrine.
And unappeased, we were for sure – no,
  downright combative –
But peregrine? That not so much. The likelihood
  we'd live
To see the UK passing out of Europe had
  receded.
The deadline was undead again. We failed where
  ghosts succeeded.

But revenants come back again – it's what they
  do – in gory
Repeating re-enactments of a traumatising scene.
Yes, nothing makes the flesh crawl like a canvass
  from a Tory:
They knock on doors in sombre clothes, with
  pallid, ghoulish mien,
These dead souls locked in torment on an endless
  Halloween.
They want your vote and not (as trick-or-treaters
  do) a sweetie –
Although their many tricks have so far failed to
  get a treaty.

November started, then, with Boris blinking in
  the ditch,
Still very much alive ('Another broken promise,' said
  The Opposition leader), in the situation which
He'd vowed would never happen. We'd not
  Brexited. Instead
We'd three more months of parliamentary
  wrangling ahead.

But at last he had the polling day he couldn't get
  before.
Now he was done, he had not done, for – eye-roll –
  he had more.

Last month a Banksy painting sold for near ten
  million quid –
It showed the House of Commons filled with
  grinning chimpanzees.
A bellwether, perhaps, of how the public wanted rid
Of pretty much the whole incumbent roster of
  MPs.

Guy Fawkes's plot had just the same idea, but,
   brethren, please:
The ballot not the Armalite. It matters to
   remember:
We cheer a *failed* mass homicide at this time in
   November.

And giving succour to the lazy cynics who believe
That all MPs are grifters, I am conscious I defame
Rudd, Letwin, Cooper, Phillips, Soubry,
   Greening, Benn and Grieve
And many others who refused to play the party
   game;
These honourable members give the Commons a
   good name.
No good deed goes unpunished, though, the
   imminent election
Adds injury to insult; first abuse, then deselection.

The starting gun was fired. Runners hurtled from
   the traps.
Each faction now made haste to sabotage its own
   campaign.

So Farage strafed the Tories, 'People's Vote' all but
  collapsed,
While UKIP lost its leader: Richard 'make your
  own jokes' Braine
Threw in the towel. (Oh, Dicky, will ye no' come
  back again?)
The Lib Dems, meanwhile, all began to
  hyperventilate:
Why couldn't nice Jo Swinson be in ITV's debate?

At least she carried on the fight. A number of
  her sex
Left politics for good, and who can blame them?
  What's the use
Of standing for a job where all the distaff staff
  expects
To drown in online hatred from the pestilential
  sluice
Of trolls, mansplaining, death threats and
  misogynist abuse?
I doubt they'll take up telly, though, for even now,
  it's funny:
Samira Ahmed's male peers earn seven times her
  money.

All patriotic rugby fans descended on the sofa,
In hopes the gods of rugby'd show the England
 team a sign:
Webb Ellis could be coming home before the day
 was over.
We ended up in second place, though not for
 want of tryin',
But here (as in much else) we couldn't get it past
 the line.

Cut off the phone. Prevent the dog from barking.
  Stop the clocks.
We're mourning now. Our rugby team got
  hammered by the 'boks.

If metaphor-for-everything is going to be our
   game
Then Bonfire Night does nicely for our
   internecine clashes.
So something that took months to build is fast
   consumed by flame,
And hot potatoes – foiled again! – are
   smouldering in the ashes,
As fortunes spent on fireworks dissolve in bangs
   and flashes.
Excitement over – dark again – you catch your
   throat and choke
On all that's left, the bitter drift of acrid-smelling
   smoke.

December

The bookshop browser lighting on this page
    may well have tumbled
To something rather obvious: I'm writing in
    advance.
It's not yet Christmas. Here's 'December'.
    Gotcha, Leith: you're rumbled!
But books take time to publish, and if I'm to have
    a chance
Of coming out before I'm out of date, I have to
    dance
A little round the timings. I intended no
    deception:
The Christmas gift book waits for no man; this is
    no exception.

So here's a chance to stocktake, and to say 'Go,
    litel book!'
For light verse isn't very much in fashion
    nowadays.
Folk don't queue up for couplets, are not avid for
    a look

On day of publication at how Pam Ayres turns a
  phrase.
How do we not love formal verse? Ah! Let me
  count the ways …
But still, in apologia, I set out my position:
My doggerel aspires to join an honourable
  tradition.

My model, first of all, was Auden's 'Letter to
  Lord Byron',
A poem filled with 'news about the England of
  the day':
Before we all had CNN, this light iambic
  chyron
Would scroll beneath the world's great rage and
  duly fade away;
Make nothing happen, right enough, but give
  him space to say
Some wry things from the sidelines. It could be a
  way of using
The trip and twang of verse to make dismaying
  news amusing.

And personal. For Auden isn't singing to the Muse
But writing to an honoured predecessor in his tomb.
I like that notion. After all, whatever pomp we use,
The word is not eternal, and it's safest to assume
That all inscriptions suffer Ozymandias's doom.

So here I bow the head, in humbly dedicating this
To 'good alike at grave and gay', 'il miglior', Uncle
  Wiz.

But Auden wrote to Byron as an equal; while
  between us
Is not so much a 'mind the gap' as 'watch for the
  crevasse'.
I can't do Auden's slalom turns, so wrote this in
  fourteeners
In the hopes four extra syllables per line would
  save my ass.
I've kept his stanza, though: rhyme royal always
  was a gas.
In 'Carpool Karaoke', then, consider me James
  Corden,
My singalonga verse form nicked from Chaucer
  via Auden.

Their honourable company, an't please you, I
  augment
With this salute to other men to whom I am
  a debtor:

Pope, Skelton, Juvenal; the arsy-versy regiment.
Clive James is still alive. Perhaps I'll write old
    Clive a letter.
I like to think he'd like this project. He'd have
    done it better.
(The critics may refer to these when they give
    me a hiding:
'I've read Augustan poets, bruv – and bruv, you
    ain't no Dryden.')

I'm 'writing to the moment', though, so what I
  lack in art
Is offset – so I hope – by the 'fierce urgency of
  now'.
My measures take the measure of a Britain come
  apart:
And seek to scribble, on the hoof, some footnotes
  as to how
Bedazzled by some 'magic beans' we sold the
  family cow.
We miss the bigger picture while we're hacking
  through the weeds:
Just where does Brexit come in Maslow's
  hierarchy of needs?

I'm biased, then. You noticed? Well. You have me
  bang to rights.
I don't like what is happening. I don't like that
  I see
A situation where, by any reasonable lights,
A country that was peaceable and prosperous and
  free
Descended to a pit of rage and demagoguery,

Where blatant lies have currency, and broken and
   marooned
Our polity lies bleeding from a self-inflicted wound.

But I am biased, also, in a more unusual way:
It wasn't ideology that made me growl and curse
When Tories moved as one to overthrow Theresa
   May.
She's two iambs, and rhymes well. Boris Johnson's
   – just *qua* verse –
Trochaic, rhymes with nothing, so is infinitely
   worse.
(If Gove or Leadsom got it, I'd have had a better
   run
And had they chosen Hunt I could have really
   had some fun.)

And metre too! I'd hoped to get a stanza from
   that chain
Of well-known pizza restaurants that threatened
   to be shut –
But couldn't make its name scan, so my hopes
   were all in vain.

You may make history, change the world, bring
empires kneeward, but
Should your name be an anapaest, you will not
make the cut.
My poem, like my father's house, contains so
many mansions –
But entry's barred to anyone who doesn't fit the
scansion.

So disregard me – after all, it's only comic verse.
We're *unacknowledged* legislators. That goes with
    the turf,
As Shelley warned us. Anyway, as fates go there
    are worse.
If I can land a gag or two I'll think I've proved
    my worth.
This is a most unserious house, built on unserious
    earth.
And fittingly, it strikes me in my *haut–remainer*
    bubble
That unacknowledged legislation's most of this
    year's trouble.

Retour eternel! Nothing's changed. We end right
    where we started.
As you read this we're probably contesting an
    election
But sure as shizzle Brexit Britain will not have
    departed.
A brand-new House will still most likely offer
    the reflection
Of a country that's incapable of choosing a direction.

What doesn't make you stronger, folks, may also
   fail to kill ya:
And so we twitch our mantle blue, for pastures
   long familiar.

Acknowledgements

*S*am would like to thank Edith Pritchett first of all for her wonderful cartoons. Also: Georgia Garrett; Rowan Yapp and all at Square Peg; Ben Schott for encouragement and advice; Alice, Marlene, Max, Jonah and Henry for emotional sustenance; and George Osborne for making this book possible – first by losing the referendum and second by giving me the sack.